# LET'S INVESTIGATE
# Triangles

# LET'S INVESTIGATE
## Triangles

By Marion Smoothey

Illustrated by Ted Evans

**MARSHALL CAVENDISH**
NEW YORK · LONDON · TORONTO · SYDNEY

**Library Edition Published 1993**

© Marshall Cavendish Corporation 1993

Published by Marshall Cavendish Corporation
2415 Jerusalem Avenue
PO Box 587
North Bellmore
New York 11710

Series created by Graham Beehag Book Design

**Library of Congress Cataloging-in-Publication Data**

Smoothey, Marion, 1943-
   Triangles / by Marion Smoothey; illustrated by Ted Evans.
     p. cm.. -- (Let's Investigate)
   Includes index.
   Summary: Introduces triangles through a combination of theory
and problems.
   ISBN 1-85435-461-2  ISBN 1-85435-455-8 (set)
   1. Triangle -- Juvenile literature. [1. Triangle] I. Evans, Ted ill.  II. Title.
   III. Series: Smoothey, Marion, 1943-  Let's Investigate.
   QA482.S67  1992                      92-12156
   516.2---dc20                     CIP
                                      AC

Printed in Singapore by Times Offset PTE Ltd
Bound in the United States

# Contents

For some of the activities in this book, you will need a compass and a protractor.

You will also need a set square. If you do not have one, you can make one from thin cardboard. A used greeting card will do.

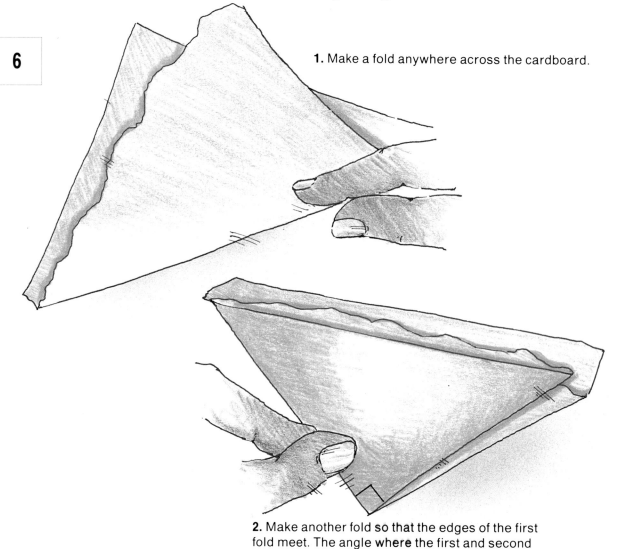

**1.** Make a fold anywhere across the cardboard.

**2.** Make another fold so that the edges of the first fold meet. The angle where the first and second folds meet is a right angle.

Use a ruler and sharp pencil to draw straight lines.

Draw diagrams in pencil and label them in ink.

# Making Triangles

On a piece of scrap paper, mark three points which are not in a straight line. Using a ruler, join the points with three straight lines. You have made a special kind of **triangle.**

A triangle is three points joined by lines. Try marking three points on a ball or an orange, and join them with three lines. You can make a triangle which has curved lines. Fasten several rubber bands over a ball so that they cross over each other. Find the triangles that they make.

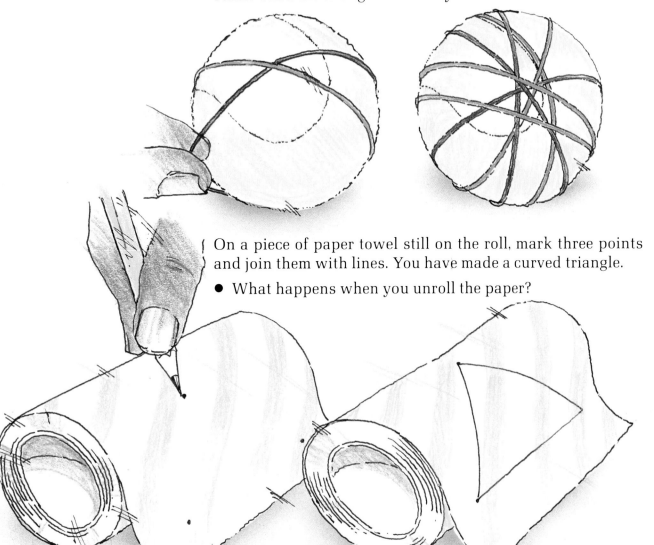

On a piece of paper towel still on the roll, mark three points and join them with lines. You have made a curved triangle.

● What happens when you unroll the paper?

On scrap paper, trace a circular object, such as the top of a can. Cut out the circle. Fold the circle in half. The fold line marks the **diameter** of the circle.

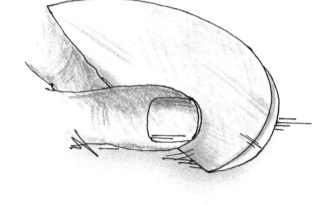

**8**

Make a mark on the **circumference**. Fold from the mark to one end of the diameter fold.

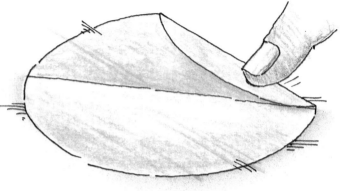

Make another fold from the point on the circumference to the other end of the diameter.

● What shape do the three fold lines make?

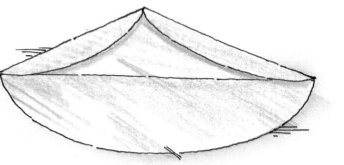

Repeat with a different sized circle.

**Keep your circle triangles.**
**You will need them later.**

# Looking for Triangles

Look around the room and out of the window. How many triangles can you see?

● How many triangles can you see in this picture?

◇ Make a copy of this table.

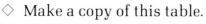

|  | **Number of Triangles** | **Number of Other Shapes** |
|---|---|---|
| 1 fold | | |
| 2 folds | | |
| 3 folds | | |
| 4 folds | | |
| 5 folds | | |
| 6 folds | | |

You need six different colored pencils and several pieces of tablet paper.

Follow the flow chart.

10

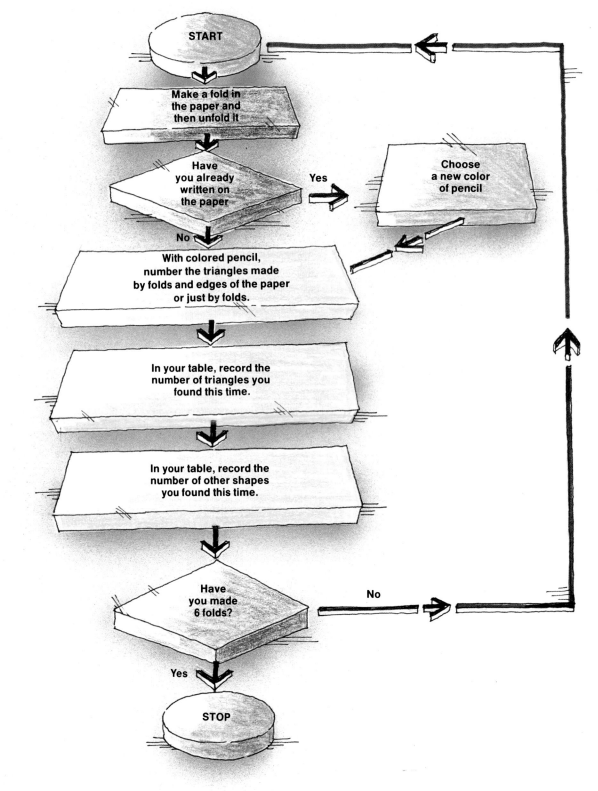

START

Make a fold in
the paper and
then unfold it

Have
you already
written on
the paper

Yes

Choose
a new color
of pencil

No

With colored pencil,
number the triangles made
by folds and edges of the paper
or just by folds.

In your table, record the
number of triangles you
found this time.

In your table, record the
number of other shapes
you found this time.

Have
you made
6 folds?

No

Yes

STOP

Repeat the investigation with several other pieces of paper. You will need a new table each time.

● What is the least number of triangles you can make with six folds?

● What is the greatest number of triangles you can make with six folds?

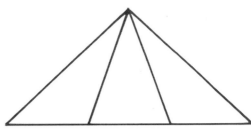

● How many triangles can you see in this diagram?

If you think that the answer is three, then you're not looking hard enough!

## Match this

● Arrange nine matches like this, to make three triangles. Move three matches to make five triangles.

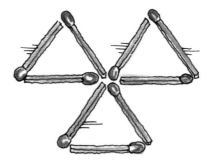

# Moving Around a Circle

◇ Trace around a circular object such as the top of a tin can. Choose three directions such as:

(Each change of direction has to be more than a quarter turn from the one before.)

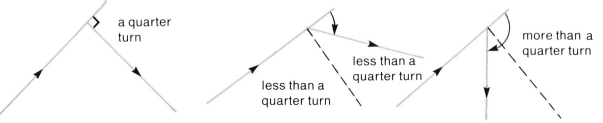

a quarter turn

less than a quarter turn

less than a quarter turn

more than a quarter turn

Mark a starting point on the **circumference** of the circle. With a ruler and pencil, draw a line in the first direction until your pencil touches the circumference at another point.

From this point on the circumference, draw a line in the second direction until it meets the circumference at another point.

Draw the third line in the third direction.

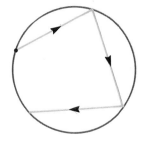

Now repeat the procedure. Start from where the third line ends. Draw a line in the first direction, then one in the second direction and so on.

It is important to keep exactly the same directions. Make sure that the fourth line is **parallel** to the first.

A set square will help you to draw parallel lines.

- Investigate what happens. Draw different sized circles and try different combinations of directions.
- Can you predict where the pattern will stop?
- How many triangles will there be?
- What happens if you use quarter turns or less?

# Odd One Out

In each of these large triangles, one of the small triangles is different from the others. Find the odd one out in each diagram.

**14**

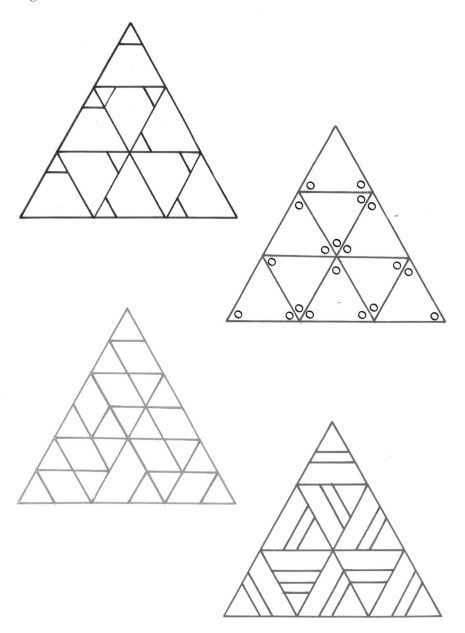

# Answers to Looking for triangles

There are at least 64 triangles in the picture.

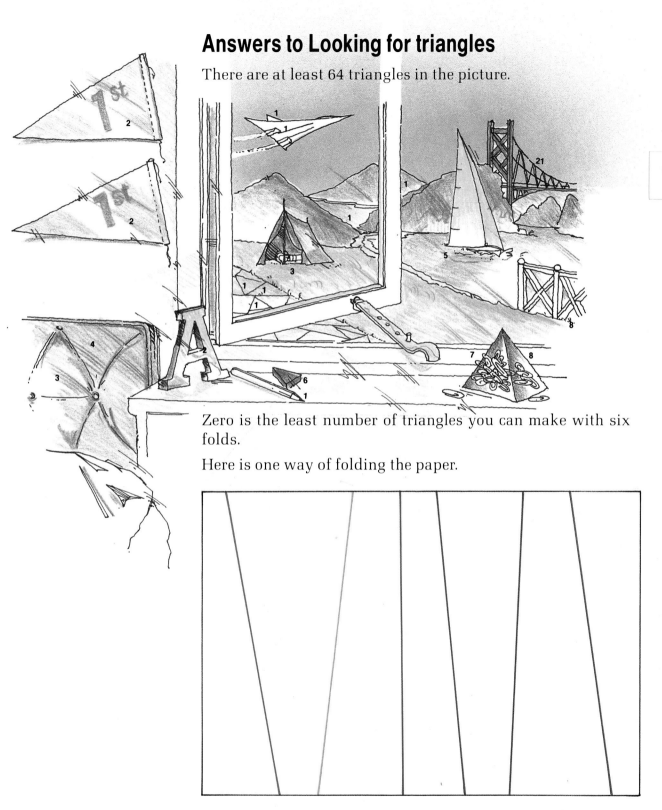

Zero is the least number of triangles you can make with six folds.

Here is one way of folding the paper.

If you use paper with straight edges, this is one way of making twenty nine triangles. Did you beat that?

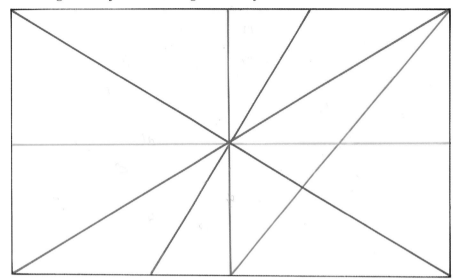

There are six triangles in the diagram.

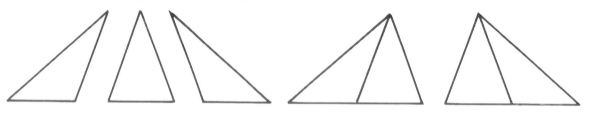

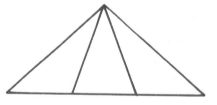

# Answer to Match this.

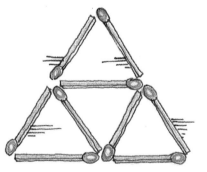

4 small triangles + 1 large.

## Answers to moving around a circle

You should have gotten results similar to these. The lines return to the starting point. It takes two sets of three lines. The lines form four triangles each time.

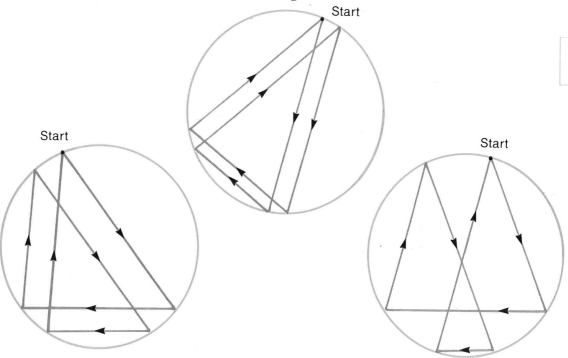

If you turn less than a quarter turn, you get stuck on the circumference.

If you turn exactly a quarter turn, you get three sides of a rectangle. When you go back over the last line you get stuck on the circumference.

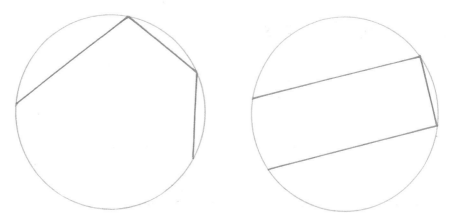

# Triangles in a Square

## Investigation 1

You need $\frac{1}{2}$ inch graph paper which you can cut up. Draw a 1 inch square. Mark with dots the corners of the $\frac{1}{2}$ inch squares (nine dots).

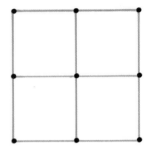

Join any three of the dots to make a triangle. Cut out the triangle. Draw another square and fit the triangle into it, in a different position.

Each of the points of the triangle must touch one of the points marked on the square. You are allowed to flip the triangle over and to turn it around.

● Draw the new position of the triangle in the square.

● Draw another square. Find another position in it for the triangle. Draw in the triangle.

● Repeat this, until you have drawn all the possible positions of the triangle in separate drawings. If you work around the square a piece at a time, you are less likely to miss any possibilities.

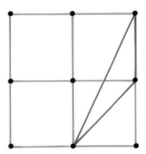

Allowed

● When you have found all the positions for the triangle, draw another square and repeat the process with a **different** triangle. See how many possible positions there are.

● Try with several different triangles.

● How many different drawings are possible for each triangle?

● Can you tell how many different drawings there will be for a particular triangle?

**Keep your drawings. You will need them later.**

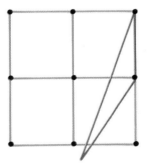

Not Allowed

# Naming Triangles and Angles

A triangle has three sides, three **vertices** and three **interior** angles. The sides are usually straight lines. The vertices are the points where the lines meet. Interior angles are the angles made inside the triangle when the sides meet at the vertices.

It is common to identify a triangle by placing a capital letter on each of the vertices. Usually, the letters follow in alphabetical order.

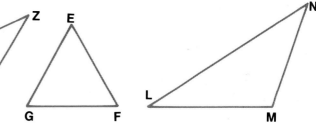

The three angles can be identified in two ways.

**1.** An angle can be called by the lower case letter that matches the letter of its vertex.

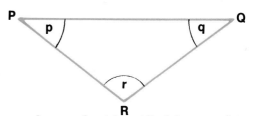

2. An angle can be identified by combining the letters of the two sides that form it and using an angle sign. The angle sign is ∠.

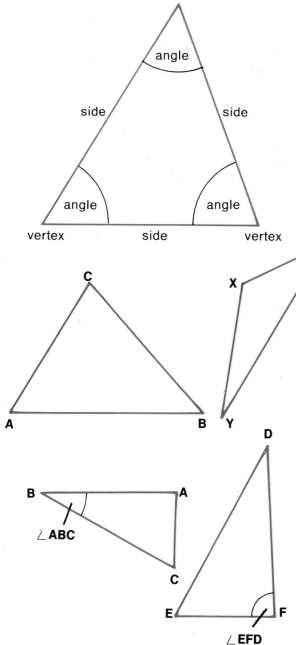

# Kinds of Triangles

## Equilateral triangles

● **1.** Measure the three sides of each of these triangles. What do you notice?

● **2.** With a protractor, measure the three interior angles of each of these triangles. What do you notice?

Triangles with all three sides the same length are called **equilateral**. The three angles of an equilateral triangle are also equal.

The equal sides and angles are marked like this.

**3.** How many of these equilateral triangles

fit into this **hexagon**

and this **rhombus**?

## Isosceles triangles

● **1.** Measure the sides of these triangles. What do you notice?

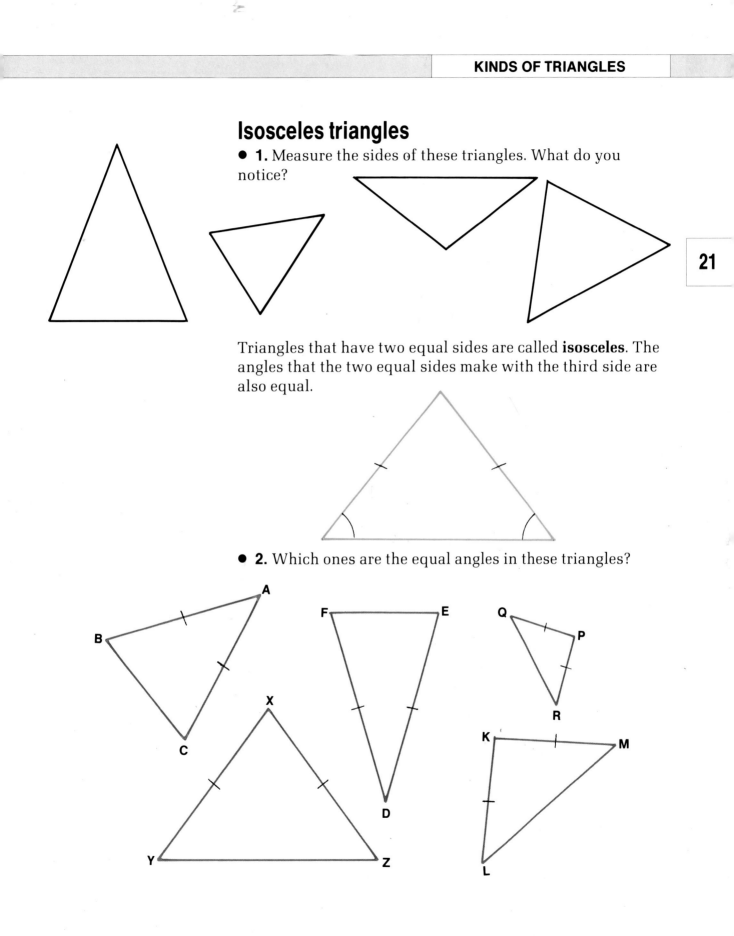

21

Triangles that have two equal sides are called **isosceles**. The angles that the two equal sides make with the third side are also equal.

● **2.** Which ones are the equal angles in these triangles?

## Scalene triangles

Triangles that are not equilateral or isosceles are called
**scalene**.

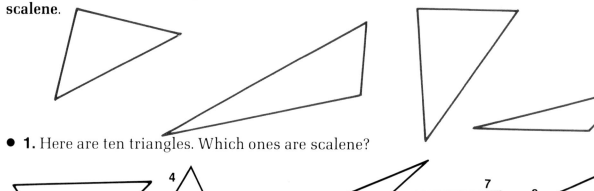

● **1.** Here are ten triangles. Which ones are scalene?

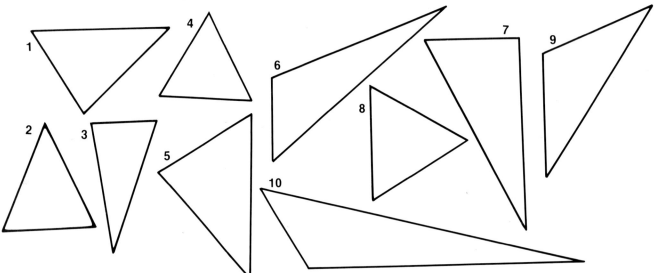

## Acute-angled triangles

An **acute** angle is one that is less than 90 degrees. Triangles
in which each of the three angles are less than 90 degrees are
acute-angled triangles.

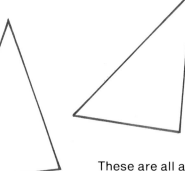

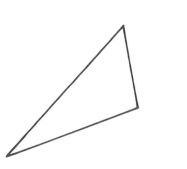

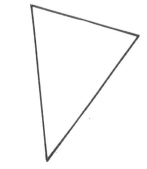

These are all acute-angled triangles.

● **2.** Are equilateral triangles acute-angled triangles?

## Obtuse-angled triangles

An **obtuse** angle is greater than 90 degrees and less than 180 degrees. A triangle in which one of the angles is greater than 90 degrees is called an obtuse-angled triangle.

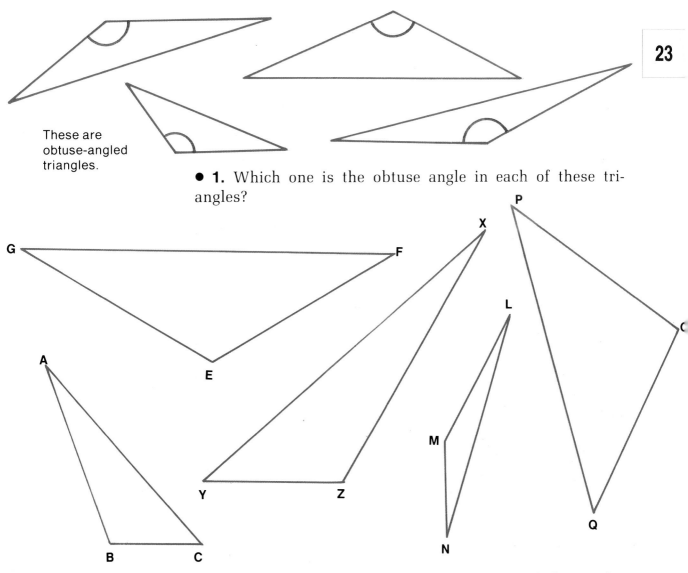

These are obtuse-angled triangles.

● **1.** Which one is the obtuse angle in each of these triangles?

● **2.** Can an isosceles triangle be an obtuse-angled triangle? Try to draw one.

● **3.** A **reflex** angle is one that is greater than 180 degrees. Try to draw a triangle with an **interior** reflex angle. What happens?

# Right-angled triangles

● **1.** With a protractor, measure the three angles of these triangles. What is the same about each of the triangles?

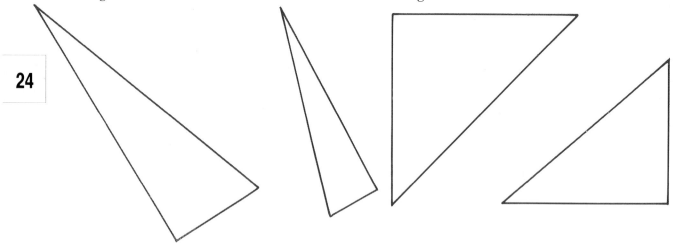

Triangles in which one of the angles is a **right angle** are called **right-angled** triangles.

◇ Draw a right-angled isosceles triangle.

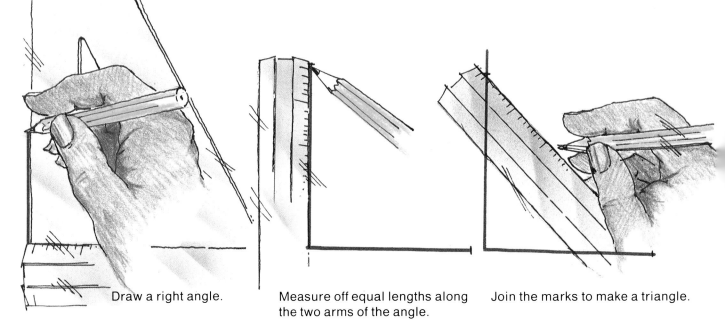

Draw a right angle.    Measure off equal lengths along    Join the marks to make a triangle.
the two arms of the angle.

● **2.** How many degrees are each of the equal angles?

● **3.** Can a right-angled triangle be equilateral?

24

# More Triangles in a Square

## Answers to Investigation 1

For some triangles, there are four possible ways they will fit into the square.

For others there are eight ways.

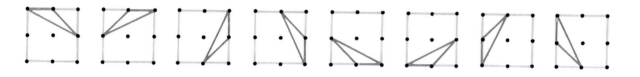

If every side of the triangle is longer than half of a side of the square, there will be four ways the triangle will fit into the square – one for each side of the square.

If any side of the triangle is shorter than half of a side of the square, there will be eight ways the triangle will fit in the square – two for each side of the square.

## Investigation 2

● How many **different** triangles can you draw using the same 1 inch square with nine points? This time, count the same triangle in different positions as only one triangle.

This counts as one triangle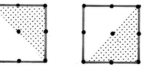

**Keep your drawings. You will need them later.**

# Circles and Triangles

**1.** Draw a circle using a compass. Keep the compass set at the same **radius** and draw another circle to **intersect** at two points with the first circle.

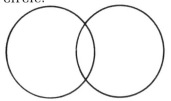

Draw a triangle by joining the centers of each circle to each other and to one of the points of intersection.

● What kind of triangle did you just make?

**2.** Draw a circle using a compass. Keep the radius the same. Place the compass point on the circumference of the first circle. Draw another circle to intersect at two points with the first circle.

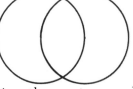

Make a triangle by joining the centers and drawing a radius from each center to one of the points of intersection.

● What kind of triangle is this?

**3.** Using a compass, draw two intersecting circles of different radii.

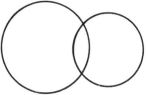

Join the centers. Draw a radius from each center to one point of intersection.

● What kind of triangle have you made?

## Answers to how many different triangles in a square

If you use the nine points, there are eight different triangles you can draw. Here they are.

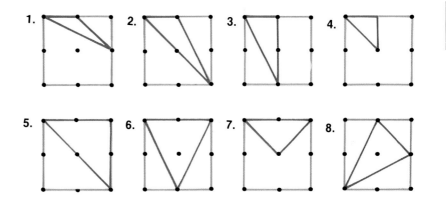

If you think you have found more, look carefully. Remember that you may have drawn the same triangle in different positions in the square.

● Test yourself to see if you remember the different kinds of triangle. Write down the correct name of each of the eight triangles in the diagrams above.

> **Look at the answer page to check your answers to pages 26 and 27. If you have gotten them all right, you may skip the next page.**

● Copy these drawings exactly. Color the scalene triangles red, the equilateral triangles black, the isosceles triangles yellow and the right-angled triangles blue. Which triangles will be green?

**28**

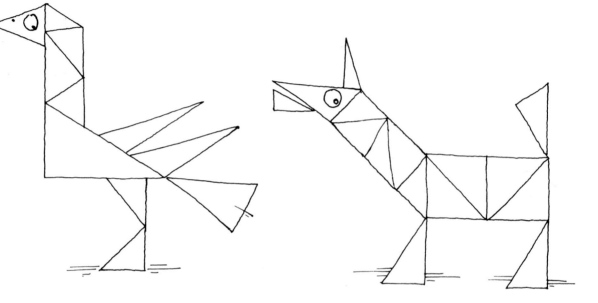

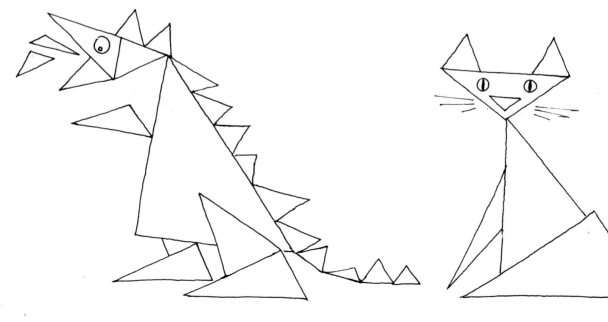

# Degrees in a Triangle

**29**

There are 360 degrees in a complete circle. If you stand facing a particular object, and then keep turning until you are back looking at the object again, you have turned 360 degrees.

This ice dancer is spinning through 360°.

In a half circle there are 180 degrees.

On a piece of scrap paper, draw a large triangle. Tear off the corners of the triangle and fit them together like the pieces of a jigsaw puzzle. Do the same for several more triangles.

● **1.** What do you notice?

● **2.** How many degrees do you think the angles of a triangle add up to?

## Answers to kinds of triangles

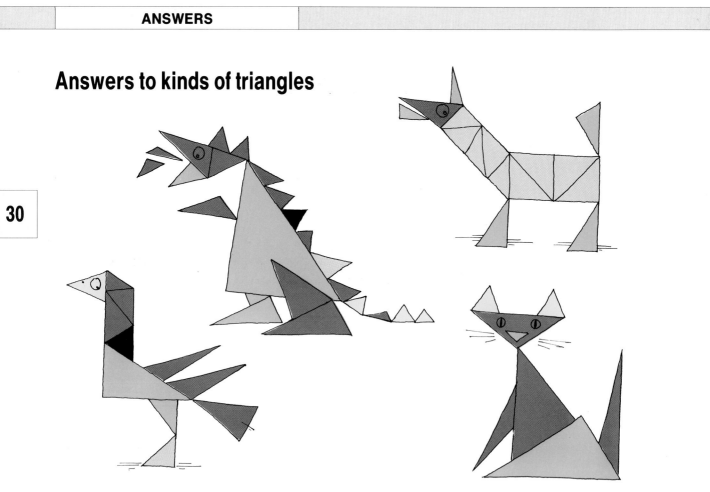

The right-angled isosceles triangles will be green.
(yellow + blue = green)

## Triangles in semicircles

Look again at the triangles you made by folding circles.

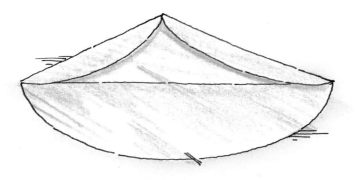

● What kind of triangles are they?

## Answers to degrees in a triangle

When you tore the corners off your triangles and fitted them together, you should have found that the three pieces fit along a straight line each time.

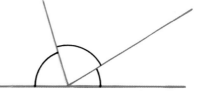

**This suggests that the three angles of a triangle add up to 180 degrees or two right angles.**

## Is seeing believing?

Tearing off the angles of a triangle and joining them to make a straight line is a demonstration that the angles of a triangle joined together equal half a circle, but it is not a proof.

Things are not always as they seem. Look carefully at the two drawings below. You can see that the pieces of the triangle on the left have been rearranged to fit into the triangle on the right.

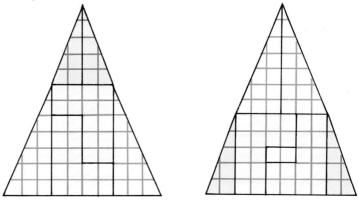

If you count the squares, the pieces and the triangles of both drawings seem to be the same size. So it is very strange that the pieces do not fill the triangle on the right. There is an empty space in the middle.

● Can you explain what has happened?

☆ **Hint - it helps to examine the triangles with a ruler.**

Another problem with the demonstration is that it only holds for the actual triangles from which you tore off the corners. It is, however, possible to prove that the angles of **any** triangle total 180 degrees.

## A reminder about angles and parallel lines

**32**

## Vertically opposite angles

When two lines intersect, the angles that are opposite to each other must be equal.

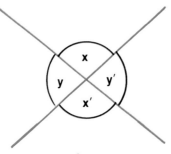

In the diagram you can see that $x + y = 180$ degrees (because they make a straight line) but $x + y' = 180$ degrees (because they make a straight line as well) therefore $y = y'$

You can prove that $x = x'$, using the same method.

## Alternate or Z angles

In the diagram you can see that a line drawn across parallel lines forms alternate angles **c** and **c'**. These are sometimes called Z angles because of the pattern of the lines.

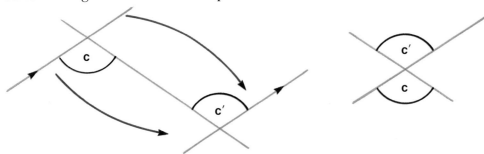

You can see that if the parallel lines were pushed together until they met, **c** and **c'** would become vertically opposite angles. This shows that alternate angles are always equal.

## Corresponding angles

A line **intersecting** with parallel lines also forms corresponding angles. These are marked a and a′ on the diagram.

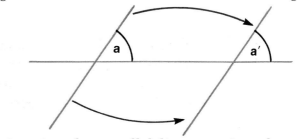

If you imagine the parallel lines moving closer and closer together until they become one line, you can see that **a** = **a**′.

**Corresponding angles are always equal.**

## A proof that the angles in any triangle total 180 degrees.

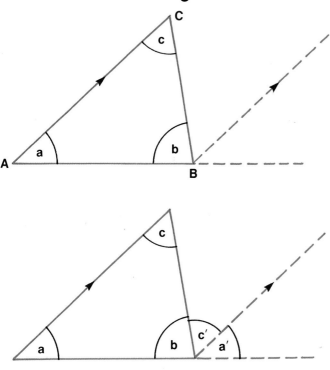

Draw a triangle ABC. Extend AB and draw a line parallel to AC through B. Label the angles **a**, **b**, and **c**.

Consider the angles **a**′ and **c**′.

Angle **a** = angle **a**′ (they are corresponding angles)

angle **c** = angle **c**′ (they are alternate angles)

but angles **b** + **c**′ + **a**′ = 180 degrees (they make a straight line)

therefore angles **a** + **b** + **c** = 180 degrees.

Because **a**, **b** and **c** can stand for any possible angles that exist: **the angles of any triangle total 180 degrees**.

# Calculating the Third Angle of a Triangle

You can use this fact to calculate the third angle of any triangle when you know the size of the other two angles.

In this triangle **ABC**, $\angle$**ABC** $= 30$ degrees, $\angle$**BAC** $= 35$ degrees.

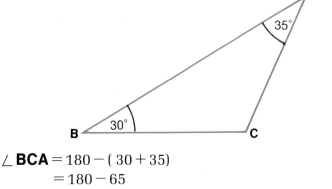

$\angle$**BCA** $= 180 - (30 + 35)$
$= 180 - 65$
$= 115$ degrees

In triangle **EFG**, $\angle$**EGF** is a right angle, $\angle$**GFE** $= 62$ degrees.

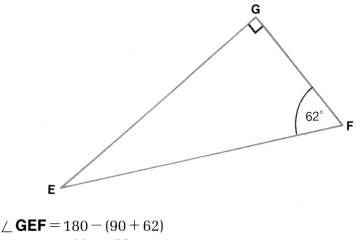

$\angle$**GEF** $= 180 - (90 + 62)$
$= 180 - 152$
$= 28$ degrees

# Calculate the third angle of these triangles.

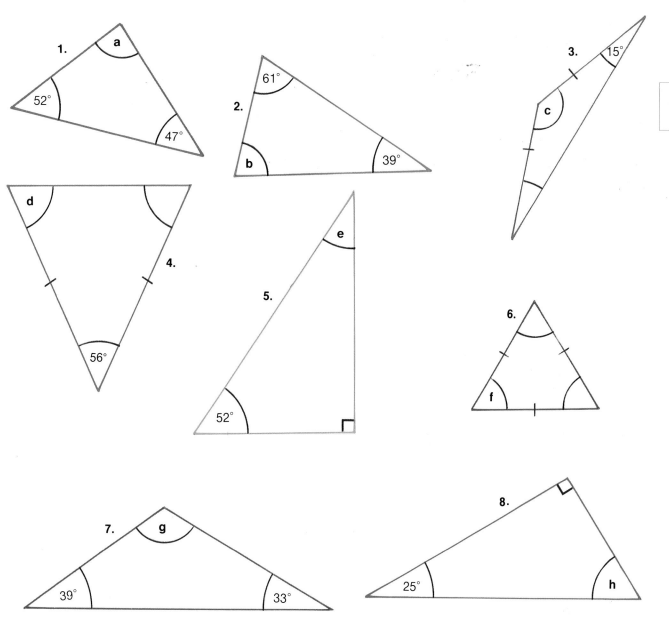

- How many degrees in each angle of any equilateral triangle?

- How many angles do you need to know to be able to find all the angles of an isosceles triangle?

# The answer to the mystery of the two triangles

If you test the triangles with a ruler, you will see that the colored pieces do not fit exactly into a triangle with straight sides.

On the first triangle, the middle piece does not quite touch the sides.

In the second triangle, the middle piece sticks out slightly past the sides.

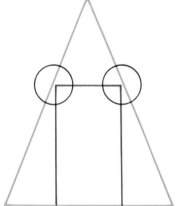

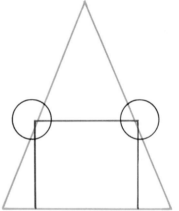

To make it work, the sides of the first triangle have to be concave, and the sides of the second triangle have to be convex.

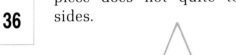

CONVEX

CONCAVE

# Constructing Triangles

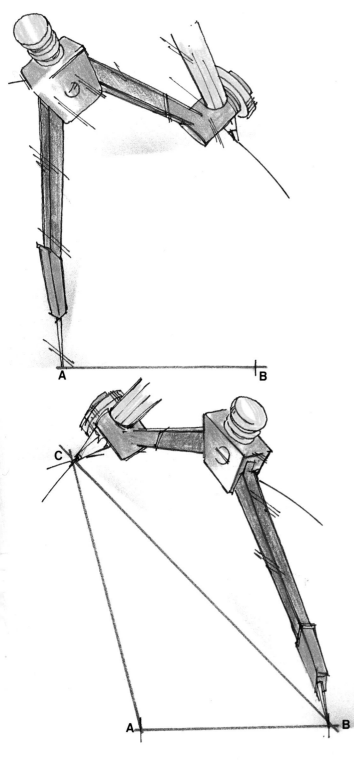

## How to draw a triangle when you know the lengths of the three sides

If you know the lengths of the three sides of a triangle, you can draw it with a compass, a sharp pencil and a ruler.

To draw a triangle with sides of 2 inches, 3 inches and 4 inches

With a ruler, draw a line. With a compass, mark off 2 inches. Mark the ends **A** and **B**.

Set the compass to 3 inches. Place the point of the compass at **A** and draw an arc.

Set the compass to 4 inches. Place the point of the compass at **B**. Draw an arc to intersect with the arc from **A**. Label the point of intersection **C**.

With a ruler, join points **A**, **B** and **C** to form a triangle.

Try drawing these triangles.
**1.** $1\frac{1}{2}$ in., 2 in. and $2\frac{1}{2}$ in.
**2.** 3 in., 4 in. and 4 in.
**3.** 5 in., $1\frac{1}{2}$ in. and 6 in.
**4.** 3 in., 3 in. and 3 in.

**Keep your drawings. You will need them later.**

# How to draw a triangle when you know the length of one side and the sizes of two angles

To draw a triangle where a side and two angles are given, always draw a sketch first and label it. You need to know the two angles at the vertices of the given line.

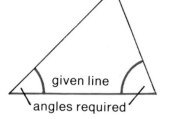

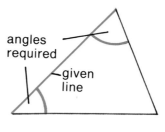

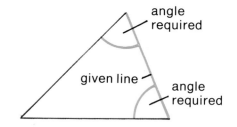

The angles you need may not be the two angles that are given. You may have to calculate the angle you need.

◇ Draw the triangle **ABC**, where **AB** $= 2\frac{1}{2}$ inches, $\angle$ **ACB** $= 35$ degrees and $\angle$ **ABC** $= 110$ degrees.

◇ First draw a labeled sketch. Be careful to write the angles in the correct positions.

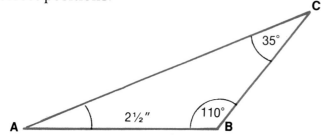

From the sketch, we can see that we have only one of the angles we need. Before we can draw the triangle, we must calculate the third angle:

$$180 - (110 + 35) = 180 - 145 = 35$$

◇ Write in the third angle on the sketch.

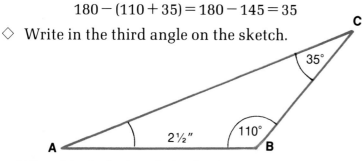

● What kind of triangle is this?

You are now ready to draw the triangle. You need a ruler, a sharp pencil and a protractor.

◇ Draw the line **AB** $2\frac{1}{2}$ inches long. Place the 0° to 180° line of the protractor along **AB** with the 90° line on **A**. With a protractor, measure 35° from A. Be careful to use the inner set of markings on the protractor. Start from 0° mark the point for 35°.

◇ With your ruler and pencil, draw a line from **A** through the 35° mark.

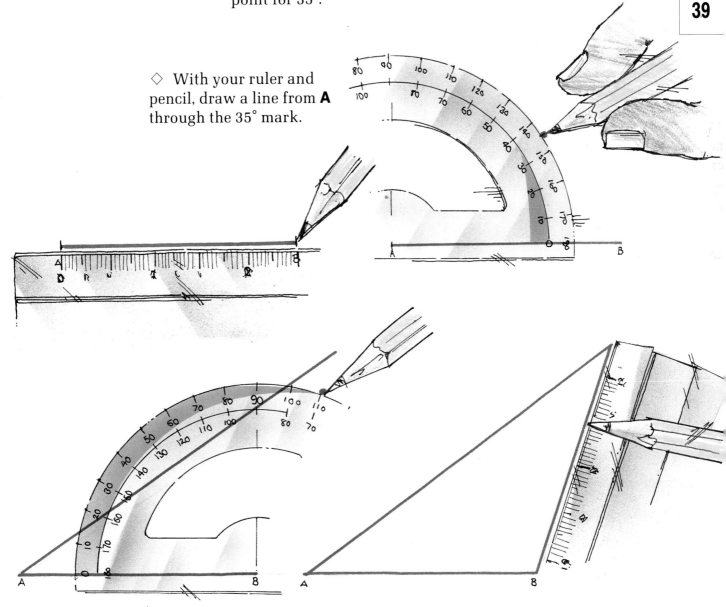

◇ Place the protractor at **B**. Measure off 110° from **B** and make a mark. This time you will need to use the outside numbers on the protractor.

◇ With a ruler and pencil, draw a line from **B** which passes through the 110° mark and meets the line that you drew from **A**. You may need to extend the line from **A**.

Your drawing should look like this.

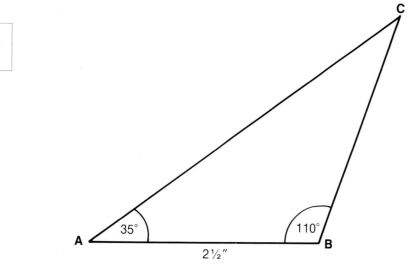

● Now try drawing these triangles. Remember to draw a labeled sketch each time.

**1.** Triangle **EFG**, **EF** = 2 in., ∠ **GEF** = 80°, ∠ **EFG** = 50°
**2.** Triangle **PQR**, **PQ** = 3 in., ∠ **PQR** = 150°, ∠ **QRP** = 17°
**3.** Triangle **LMN**, **MN** = 2 in., ∠ **NLM** = 43°, ∠ **LNM** = 85°
**4.** Triangle **RST**, **RS** = 1½ in., ∠ **TRS** = 60°, ∠ **RST** = 30°
**5.** The isosceles triangle **XYZ**, **XY** = 2 in., ∠ **ZXY** = 70°.
There are two possible answers to this.

**Keep your drawings. You will need them later.**

# Answers to drawing the triangles on page 37

Your triangles should be the same as these. It is all right if they are turned around differently on the page.

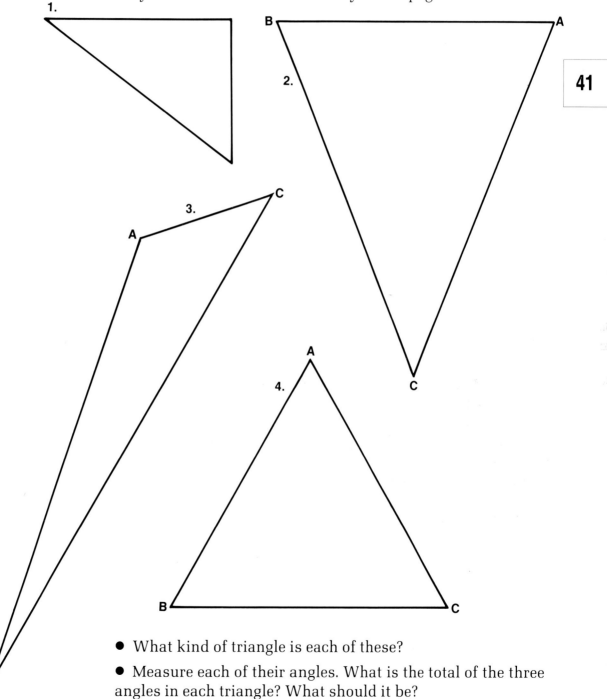

● What kind of triangle is each of these?

● Measure each of their angles. What is the total of the three angles in each triangle? What should it be?

## How to draw a triangle when you know two sides and one angle

In this situation, it is again very important to draw a labeled sketch and put on the information you are given. Usually, you can only draw the triangle if the angle you are given is the one between the two lines of which you know the lengths.

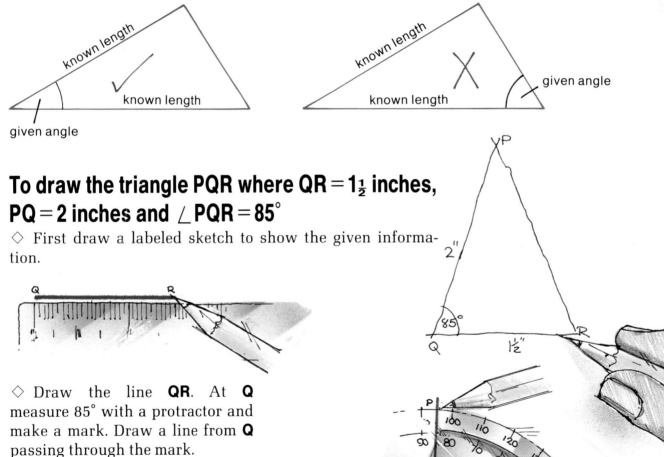

## To draw the triangle PQR where QR = 1½ inches, PQ = 2 inches and ∠PQR = 85°

◇ First draw a labeled sketch to show the given information.

◇ Draw the line **QR**. At **Q** measure 85° with a protractor and make a mark. Draw a line from **Q** passing through the mark.

◇ Measure off 2 inches along this line and mark the point **P**.

◇ With a ruler, draw a line to join **P** and **R**.

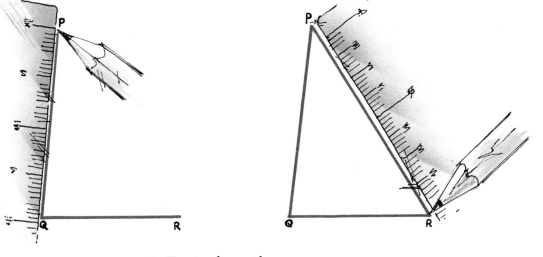

● Try to draw these:
**1.** Triangle **ABC**, **AB** = 3in., **AC** = 1 in., ∠ **BAC** = 60°
**2.** Triangle **EFG**, **EF** = $1\frac{1}{2}$ in., **FG** = 2 in., ∠ **EFG** = 35°
**3.** Triangle **JKL**, **JK** = 5 in., **JL** = 4 in., ∠ **KJL** = 10°
**4.** Triangle **MNO**, **NO** = $2\frac{1}{2}$ in., **MO** = 2 in., ∠ **NOM** = 120°

**Keep your drawings. You will need them later.**

## Challenges

**1.** Draw the isosceles triangle **ABC**, where **AB** = **AC** = 2 inches and ∠ **ABC** = 70°.

**2.** Draw the isosceles triangle **XYZ**, where **XY** = 2 inches and ∠ **XYZ** = 110°.

# The answers to drawing triangles when you are given two angles and a side

Your triangles should be the same as these. It is all right if they are turned around differently on the page.

**44**

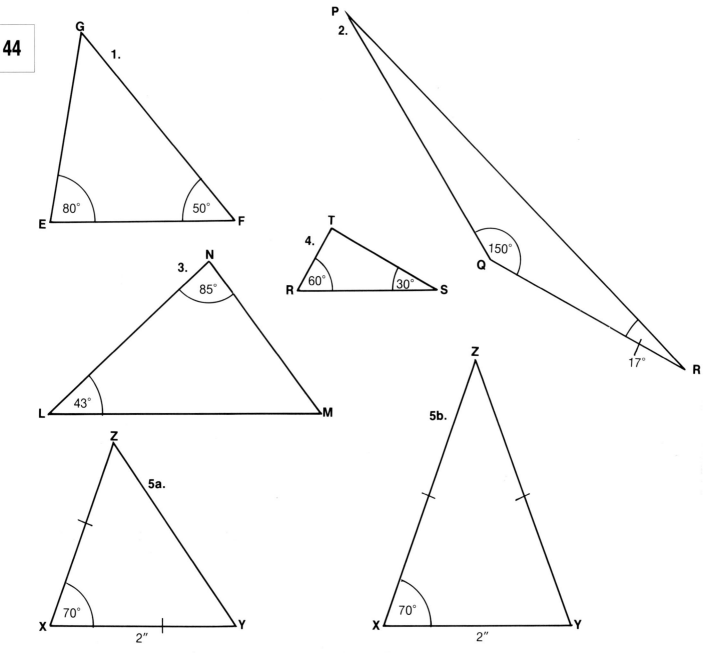

● What kind of triangles are numbers 1 through 4?

# Impossible Triangles

● **1.** What happens when you try to draw a triangle with sides of 1 inch, $1\frac{1}{2}$ inches and 3 inches?

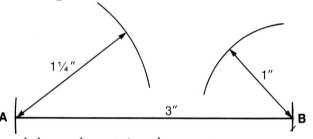

● **2.** Try and draw these triangles.
**a)** 3 in., 4 in., 5 in.  **b)** $1\frac{1}{2}$ in., $1\frac{1}{2}$ in., 4 in.  **c)** 2 in., 2 in., 5 in.
**d)** 2 in., 2 in., 3 in.  **e)** 1 in., 2 in., 3 in.

| A. Length of shortest side | B. Length of middle side | C. Length of longest side | Triangle Yes/No |
|---|---|---|---|
| 1 | $1\frac{1}{2}$ | 3 | No |

Make a table like this to record the lengths of the sides and whether or not they make a triangle.

● **3.** Look at your results carefully. Can you see a way of telling whether or not three lengths will make a triangle?

If you can't, try adding the shortest and middle sides together. Put in another column at the end of your table. In it, record whether or not the total length of the shortest and middle sides is longer than the longest side.

| A. Length of shortest side | B. Length of middle side | C. Length of longest side | Triangle Yes/No | A+B>C Yes/No |
|---|---|---|---|---|
| 1 | $1\frac{1}{2}$ | 3 | No | No |

(> means "greater than")

● **4.** Without drawing them, say which of these lines will make triangles.
**a)** 4 in., 5 in., 6in.
**b)** 4 in., 5 in., 10 in.
**c)** 1 in., 1in., 5 in.
**d)** 6 in., $\frac{3}{4}$in., $5\frac{1}{2}$ in.
**e)** 5 in., 10 in., 5 in.

# Answers to drawing triangles when you know two sides and one angle

If you cut out your drawings, they should fit exactly on top of these.

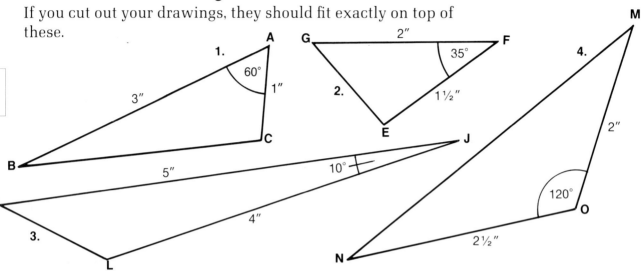

You were not given enough information to draw triangle 5.

# Answers to the challenges on page 43

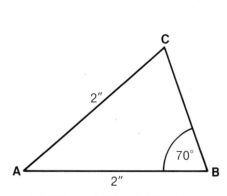

∠**ABC** = ∠**ACB** = 70° (they are the angles where the two equal sides of an isosceles triangle meet the third side)

∠**CAB** = 180 − (2 × 70) = 40°

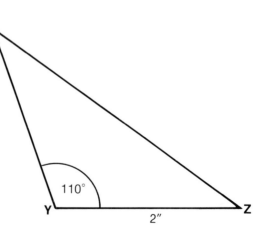

There cannot be another angle of 110° – this would make more than 180°. Therefore the two equal angles must be ∠**XZY** and ∠**YXZ**. The two equal sides must be **XY** and **YZ**.

This is another kind of impossible triangle. See if you can copy it.

These drawings will help you. Draw very lightly at first, because you will have to erase some of the lines later.

**1.** Draw an equilateral triangle with 3 inch sides. You now know three ways of doing this.

**2.** At each corner, mark off ½ inch and ¼ inch along the sides of the triangle.

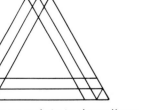

**3.** Join these points to draw lines parallel to the sides of the triangle.

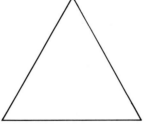
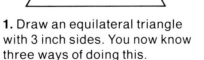

**4.** Look carefully at the original drawing to see which lines you need to erase, and erase them now.

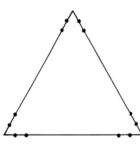

**5.** Draw in the lines you do want and color your impossible triangle.

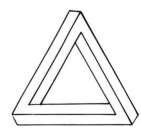

These triangles are called Penrose triangles, after a Dr. Penrose, who was the first person to study them.

# Congruent Triangles

48

When you checked your triangle drawings, you had to look to see if they were the same size and shape as the ones on the answer pages. They might be turned around a different way from yours, but you should be able to fit yours exactly on top of them.

These triangles are the same size and shape.

These triangles are not the same size and shape.

When one shape can fit exactly over another, the shapes are said to be **congruent**.

This shape is a happyhound.

● Which of these shapes are congruent with the happyhound? It helps to make a tracing of the happyhound.

Which of the triangles below are congruent to this one?

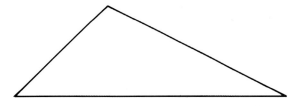

It is easier to spot them if you make a tracing of the original triangle and fit it over the others. Remember that you are allowed to turn the tracing around and flip it over.

**49**

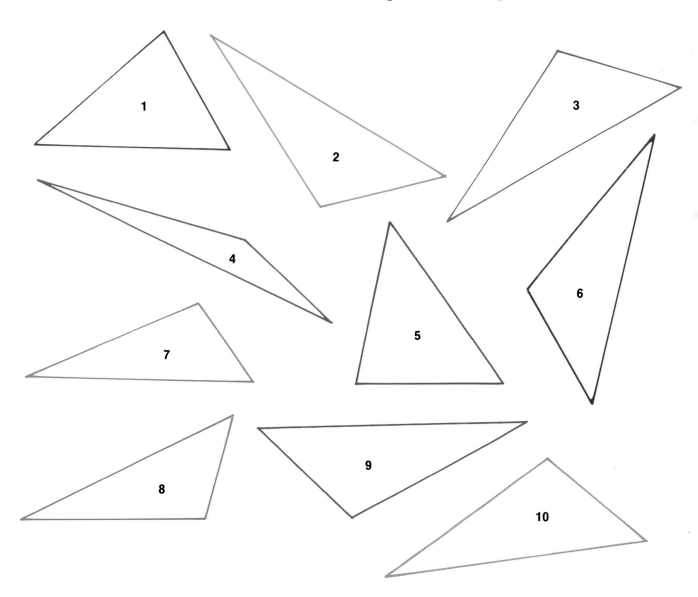

# Right-angled Triangles

**50**

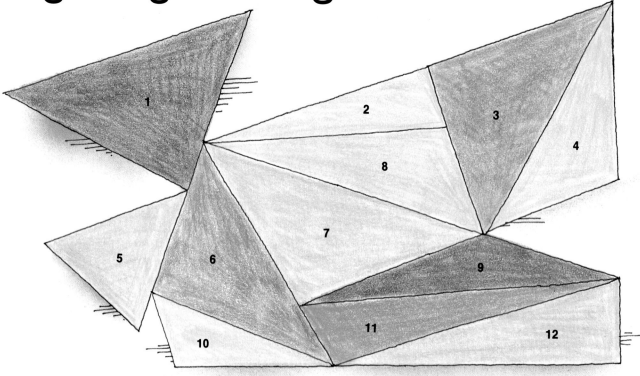

Which of these triangles are right-angled triangles? You need
a set square to check them.

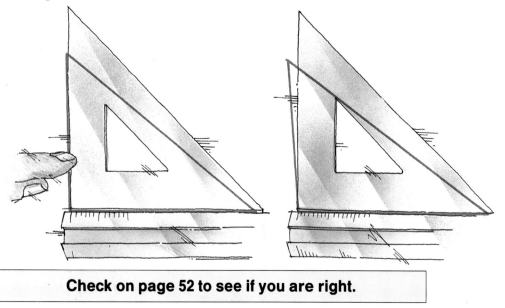

**Check on page 52 to see if you are right.**

## The Hypotenuse

The side opposite to the right angle in a right-angled triangle has a special name. It is called the **hypotenuse**.

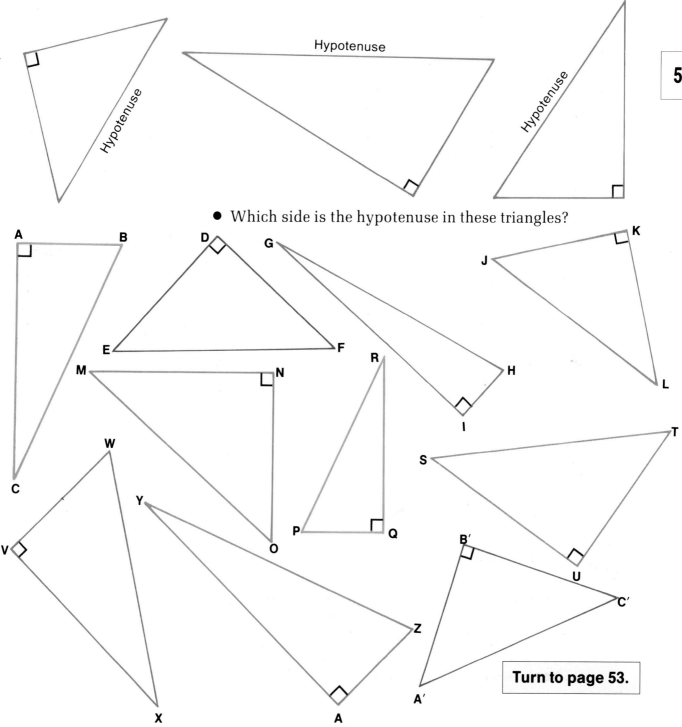

● Which side is the hypotenuse in these triangles?

**Turn to page 53.**

The right-angled triangles were 2, 3, 6 and 12. If you spotted more than three of them, and didn't say that any of the other triangles were right-angled, turn back to page 51.

Turnback to page 50 and take a look at which ones were the right-angled triangles. Use your set square to check the answers.

● You may need more practice, so try these. Again look carefully and identify the right-angled triangles. Remember that the right-angle can be in any position. Use your set square to check *all* the angles in each triangle, if you need to.

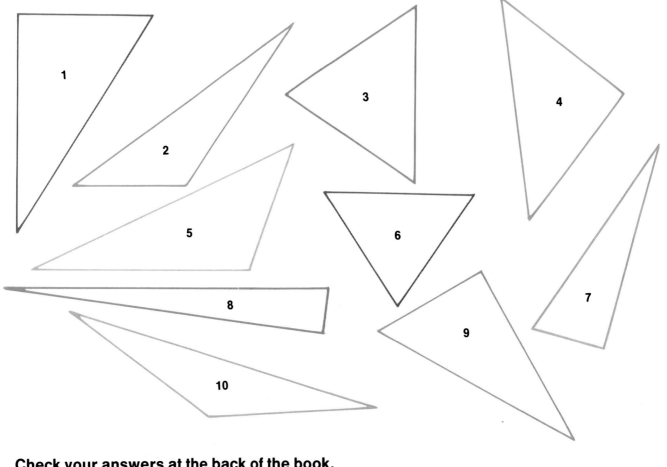

**Check your answers at the back of the book.**

**Turn back to page 51.**

The hypotenuses were **BC**, **EF**, **GH**, **JL**, **MO**, **PR**, **ST**, **WX**, **YZ**, **A′C′**.

> **If you have gotten at least eight correct answers, move straight to page 54.**

If you have gotten seven or fewer correct answers, look again at the diagrams that show you the hypotenuses of three different triangles, on page 51. You can see that the hypotenuse is the side **opposite** to the right angle. The right angles are marked with two lines to make a square at the vertex of the triangle.

**53**

● Identify the hypotenuse in each of these triangles.

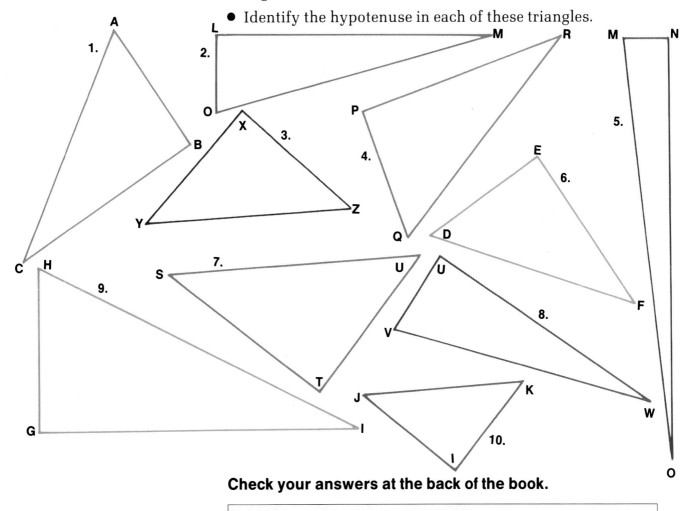

**Check your answers at the back of the book.**

> **Turn to page 54.**

# Puzzles with Squares and Right-angled Triangles

**54**

You need a set square, a ruler, three different colored pencils or felt tip pens and scissors.

## Puzzle 1

**1.** Check, with your set square, that this is a right-angled triangle.

**1.**

The side marked in red is the hypotenuse.

2. Check, with a ruler and set square, that the shape drawn on the hypotenuse in the next diagram is a square.

**2.**

**3.** Copy diagram 3 exactly on to a piece of paper. Use two colors to color it in as shown. Cut out the whole square.

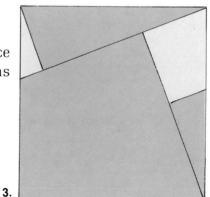

**3.**

**4.** Lay the square on top of the square in diagram 2 to check that the squares are **congruent**.

**5.** Cut the square into the five pieces made by the lines in it.

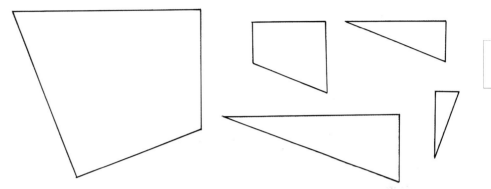

**6.** Rearrange the five pieces to make two smaller squares.

● Try to do this yourself. If you have to give up, the answer is on the next page.

**7.** Check that the two smaller squares fit on to the two shorter sides of the right-angled triangle.

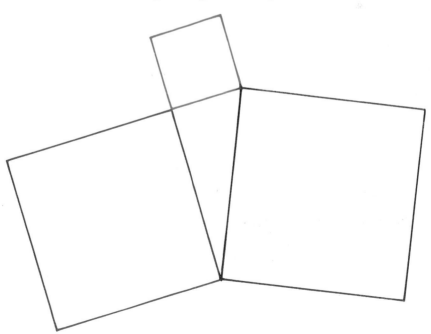

The two smaller squares were made from the large square.

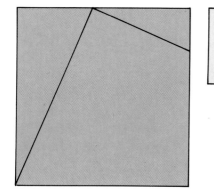 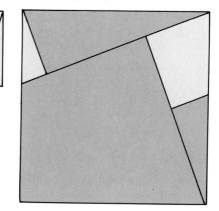

**56**

The large square fits onto the hypotenuse of the right-angled triangle. The two smaller squares fit on to the two shorter sides of the same triangle.

### THE AREA OF THE SQUARE ON THE HYPOTENUSE = THE SUM OF THE AREAS OF THE SQUARES ON THE OTHER TWO SIDES.

## Puzzle 2

**1.** In the middle of a piece of paper, draw a right-angled triangle. Use your set square and ruler to draw a square on each side of the triangle. Color the hypotenuse red. Shade each of the other two squares a different color.

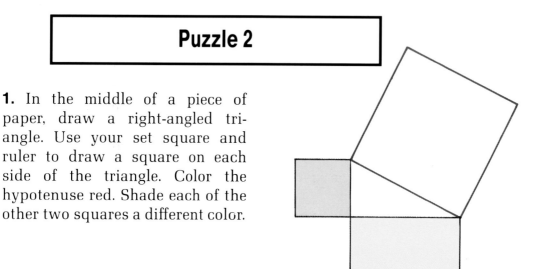

**2.** Cut off the two smaller squares. Lay them side by side as shown.

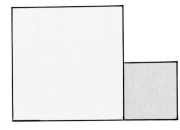

**3.** Measure the length of the bottom edge where the two squares are joined together. Halve that length. Make a mark half way along the bottom edge.

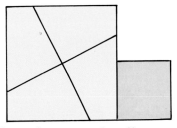

**4.** Use the same length to mark off a point on each of the other three sides of the large square. Join up the points as shown.

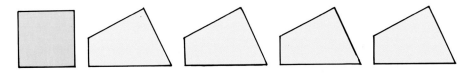

**5.** Cut the large square into four pieces along the lines. Use the small square and the four pieces of the large square to make one large square.

● Try to do this yourself. If you have to give up, the answer is on the next page.

Check that the large square you just made is **congruent** with the square on the hypotenuse of *your* original right-angled triangle.

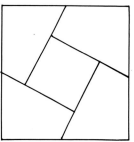

The square on the hypotenuse is made from the same pieces as the two squares on the other two sides.

● What does this tell you about the square on the hypotenuse of a right-angled triangle?

# The Rope Stretchers

Look at this triangle.

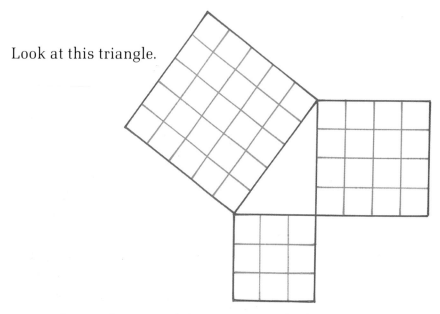

● **1.** What is the area of the square on the longest side?

● **2.** What is the combined area of the squares on the two shorter sides?

● **3.** What do you notice about your answers to 1. and 2.?

● **4.** What does this tell you about the angle opposite the 5 side?

## Making a right-angle with string

You need a piece of thin string about 14 inches long, a ruler, a pen and three thumbtacks.

With the pen, make a mark near one end of the string. Tie a knot, so that the mark is in the middle of the knot.

Measure 1 inch from the knot and make a mark. Tie a knot, so that the mark is in the middle of the knot. Repeat this, until you have made thirteen knots.

With the thumbtacks, pin down the fourth and eighth knots. Pull the first and last knots together. Pin them down.

You have made a triangle.

Count the pieces between the knots.

● **5.** What kind of triangle have you made?

● **6.** What do you know about the angle opposite the 5 side?

Thousands of years ago, the ancient Egyptians used a rope, knotted in the same way as your string, to lay out the foundations for some of the most amazing buildings ever built.

The pyramid of Khufu or the Great Pyramid, built by hundreds of thousands of slaves for King Cheops, is the largest single building ever constructed. When it was built, 4,500 years ago, it was 481 feet tall and covered nearly 13 acres at its base. It was built from about $2\frac{1}{2}$ million blocks of sandstone. The biggest block weighed 16 tons, and yet the blocks were placed exactly in their correct positions to an accuracy a tiny fraction of an inch.

# Glossary

**acute**  an acute angle is less than 90 degrees

**circumference**  the distance, or the line, around the edge of a circle

**congruent**  shapes are congruent when they are exactly the same size and shape as one another

**diameter**  the diameter of a circle is the distance, or a line, from one point on the circumference (edge) of the circle to another point on the circumference, that passes through the center of the circle. There are an infinite number of diameters in every circle. Each one bisects (cuts in half) the circle into two semicircles.

**equilateral**  having equal sides

**hexagon**  a closed shape with six sides

**hypotenuse**  the side opposite the right angle in a right-angled triangle

**interior angle**  in a triangle the interior angles are the three angles inside it

**intersect**  a line intersects with another when it crosses it

**isosceles**  having a pair of equal sides

**obtuse**  an angle of more than 90 and less than 180 degrees

**parallel**  lines that are parallel always remain the same distance apart. They will never intersect, however far they are extended. Railway tracks are pairs of parallel lines.

**radius**  the distance from the center of a circle to any point on its circumference

**reflex**  an angle of more than 180 degrees

**rhombus**  a closed shape with four equal sides

**right angle**  an angle of ninety degrees; a quarter turn

**scalene**  a scalene triangle has no equal sides

**vertex**  a vertex of a triangle is the point where two of its sides meet. A triangle has three vertices.

# Answers

**Page 7**
The triangle becomes flat, with straight lines as you unroll the paper.

**Page 8**
The three folds form a triangle.

**Page 9**
See page 15

**Page 11**
See pages 15 and 16

**Page 13**
See page 17

**Page 14**

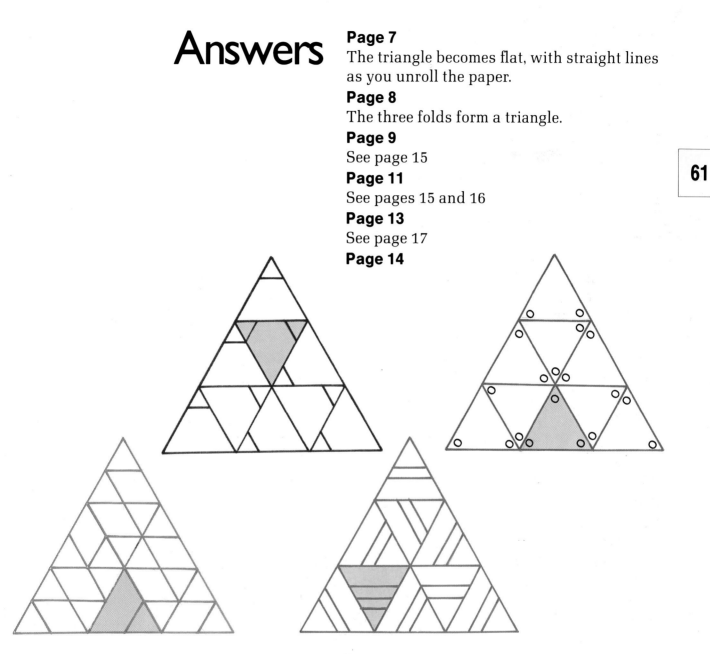

**Page 18**
See page 25

**Pages 20**
**1.** In each of the triangles, the three sides are the same length.

**2.** In each of the triangles, each of the angles measures 60°.

**3.** Six equilateral triangles fit into the hexagon and eight fit into the rhombus.

**Page 21**

**1.** In each of the triangles, two of the sides are the same length.

**2.** $\angle$ **ABC** = $\angle$ **ACB**

$\angle$ **DFE** = $\angle$ **DEF**

$\angle$ **PQR** = $\angle$ **PRQ**

$\angle$ **XYZ** = $\angle$ **XZY**

$\angle$ **KLM** = $\angle$ **KML**

**Page 22**

**1.** The scalene triangles are **1**, **3**, **5**, **5**, **6**, **7**, and **10**

**2.** Yes, equilateral triangles are acute-angled triangles.

**Page 23**

**1.** $\angle$ **GEF**, $\angle$ **ABC**, $\angle$ **YZX**, $\angle$ **LMN**, $\angle$ **POQ**

**2.** Yes, an isosceles triangle can be obtuse-angled. Here is one example.

**3.** You cannot draw a triangle with an interior reflex angle.

**Page 24**

**1.** Each of the triangles has a right angle in it.

**2.** Each of the equal angles will measure 45 degrees.

**3.** If you try to make a triangle with even *two* right angles, the sides won't meet to form a third angle.

**Page 25**

See page 27

**Page 26**

**1.** You have made an isosceles triangle.

**2.** You have made an equilateral triangle.

**3.** You have made a scalene triangle.

**Page 27**

**1.** Scalene

**2.** Scalene

**3.** Right-angled

**4.** Right-angled isosceles

**5.** Right-angled isosceles

**6.** Isosceles

**7.** Right-angled isosceles

**8.** Isosceles

**Page 28**

See page 30

**Page 29**

See page 31

**Page 30**

Any triangle in a semicircle that has the diameter as one of its sides will be a right-angled triangle.

**Page 31**

See page 36

**Page 35**

**1.** **a** = 180 − (52 + 47) = 180 − 99 = 81 degrees

**2.** **b** = 180 − (61 + 39) = 180 − 100 = 80 degrees

**3.** **c** = 180 − (2 + 15) = 180 − 30 = 150 degrees

**4.** 2 × **d** = 180 − 56 = 124

**d** = 62 degrees

**5.** **e** = 180 − (90 + 52) = 180 − 142 = 38 degrees

**6.** **f** = 180 × 3 = 60 degrees

**7.** **g** = 180 − (39 + 33) = 180 − 72 = 108 degrees

**8.** **h** = 180 − (90 + 25) = 180 − 115 = 65 degrees

The angles of any equilateral triangle are all 60 degrees.

If you know one angle of an isosceles triangle, you can calculate the other two.

**Page 37**

See page 41

**Page 38**

The triangle is isosceles.

## Page 40
See page 44
## Page 41
**1.** A right-angled triangle
**2.** An isosceles triangle
**3.** A scalene triangle
**4.** An equilateral triangle
The three angles in each triangle should add up to 180 degrees. If they don't, it is due either to inaccurate drawing or to inaccurate use of the protractor.
## Page 43
See page 46
## Page 44
**1.** An isosceles triangle
**2.** A scalene triangle
**3.** A scalene triangle
**4.** A right-angled triangle
## Page 45
**1.** The arcs do not intersect. You cannot make a triangle.
**2. and 3.** Results for table

| A. Length of shortest side | B. Length of middle side | C. Length of longest side | Triangle Yes/No | A + B > C Yes/No |
|---|---|---|---|---|
| 3 | 4 | 5 | Yes | Yes |
| 1½ | 1½ | 4 | No | No |
| 2 | 2 | 5 | No | No |
| 2 | 2 | 3 | Yes | Yes |
| 1 | 2 | 3 | No | No |

**3.** The lines will not make a triangle, unless the total length of the two shortest sides is greater than the length of the longest side.
**4. a)** Yes **b)** No **c)** No **d)** Yes **e)** No

## Page 48
Happyhound number **4** is congruent.

## Page 49
Triangles **2, 3, 6, 9,** and **10** are congruent
## Page 51
See page 53
## Page 52
The right-angled triangles are **1**, **4**, **7**, **8**, and **9**
## Page 53
**1.** AC
**2.** OM
**3.** YZ
**4.** QR
**5.** MO
**6.** DF
**7.** SU
**8.** VW
**9.** HI
**10.** JK
## Page 58
The square on the hypotenuse of a right-angled triangle is equal to the sum of the squares on the other two sides.
**1.** 25 units **2.** 16 units + 9 units = 25 units
## Page 59
**3.** They are the same.
**4.** The angle is a right angle.
**5.** It is a 3, 4, 5 triangle
**6.** The angle is a right angle.

# Index